I0059457

# Economic Growth and
# Human Welfare

# ECONOMIC GROWTH AND HUMAN WELFARE

## Conflict and Compromise

## Vernon Routley

Copyright © Vernon Routley 2021

All rights reserved. No part of this publication may be
reproduced, stored in a retrieval system or transmitted
in any form by any means, electronic, mechanical,
photocopying, recording or otherwise, without
the prior written permission of the publisher and
copyright holder. Vernon Routley  asserts the moral
right to be identified as the author of this work.

Typeset by BookPOD

Disclaimer
The material in this book is general comment only and
neither purports nor intends to be specific advice related
to any particular reader. It does not represent professional
advice and should not be relied on as the basis for any
decision or action on any matter that it covers. To the
maximum extent permitted by law, the author and
publisher disclaim all responsibility and liability to any
person or entity, whether a purchaser or not, in respect to
anything and of the consequences of anything done by any
such person in reliance, whether in whole or in part, upon
the whole or any part of the contents of this publication.

ISBN:  978-1-922270-64-1 (pbk)   eISBN:
978-1-922270-65-8 (ebook)

# CONTENTS

# CHAPTER 1

# ECONOMIC GROWTH IN PERSPECTIVE

In historical terms, the idea of economic growth as a separately identifiable concept is a relatively new one. Indeed, not until about three centuries ago did people begin to think of material progress as a desirable or even a possible condition. Before then the most that men hoped for from life was peace and prosperity. And since these conditions seldom seemed to apply to the circumstances in which they found themselves, people either tended to hark back to the 'good old days' in which they felt peace and prosperity had existed or to look forward towards a future in which they hoped such conditions would prevail.

By the early 18th century, however, it was becoming apparent to observers in northern and western Europe, and especially in Holland and Great Britain, that economic conditions were clearly improving. In 1724 the English journalist and pamphleteer Daniel Defoe began *A Tour through the Whole Island of Great Britain*. In the introduction to his subsequent book he set out its purpose as:

> 'a description of the most flourishing and opulent country in the world ... [which covers] The situation of things ... as they are; the improvements in the soil, the product of the earth, the labour of the poor, the improvement

in manufactures, in merchandises, in navigation ... [and concludes with an apology that] Even while the sheets are in the press, new beauties appear in several places and almost to every part we are obliged to add appendixes and supplemental accounts of fine houses, new undertakings, buildings, etc. and thus posterity will continually be adding; every age will find an increase in glory.'[1]

While those comments reflected the optimistic circles in which he moved, they left unanswered the issue of measurement. Three hundred years later economists are using a surrogate of economic growth, the marketplace and the goods and services traded therein. The validity

---

1    D. Defoe, *A Tour through the Whole Island of Great Britain*, P. Rogers (ed.), Webb and Bower. 1989, p. 12.

of this measure is never analysed despite the continuing inconsistencies it leads to.

# CHAPTER 2

# LIVING TO WORK OR WORKING TO LIVE

Over the past two centuries, the emergence of economic growth as a central objective of public policy represents, in itself, a 'cultural mutation'.

For most of recorded history, the central objectives of various societies, in so far as they can be descried, appear to have revolved around territorial aggrandisement or religious proselytization, with individual societies either seeking to extend their spheres of influence or to maintain their existing ones in the face of the aggressive intentions of their neighbours. The idea of economic growth as a separately identifiable concept had no place in public policy.

By the end of the 20th century, however, the pursuit of economic growth has come to have the force of a secular religion accepted without question as the appropriate goal for virtually all societies throughout the world. So much so, that in the words of one dissident economist, 'So large does [economic growth] bulk in our thoughts that we can only suppose a vacuum must remain should it be relegated to a smaller role.'[2]

---

2  J.K. Galbraith, *The Affluent Society*, Andre Deutsch, 1985, p. 102.

Yet for the more affluent societies of the world there is now a clear alternative to maximising economic growth. For, just as affluent individuals can choose between increased income or increased leisure, so also any societies above the subsistence level really have a choice between producing more or working less; between the present growth-oriented culture, wherein the central objective is to endlessly expand the output of goods and services, and a leisure-oriented culture wherein the central objective would be to increase an individual's opportunities for personal development by maximising the availability of leisure time.

Although work, rather than leisure, has always been the dominating force in economic and social life, a number of writers have, over the centuries, argued in favour of reversing the emphasis.

The Greek philosopher Aristotle, writing in the fourth century BC, argued that:

> 'it is commonly believed that to have happiness one must have leisure. We occupy ourselves in order that we may have leisure, just as we make war for the sake of peace.'[3]

Almost 2,000 years later, the English statesman and martyr Sir Thomas More wrote his account of Utopia, an island in the Southern Hemisphere where everything was done in the best possible way. It had been visited accidentally by an English sailor, one Raphael Hythloday, who having spent five years there 'returned to Europe with the express purpose of making its wise institutions known.'[4] In Utopia,

3   Aristotle, *Ethics* ( J. Thomson trans), Allen & Unwin, 1953, p. 274.

4   B. Russell, *A History of Western Philosophy*, Allen &

the magistrates 'saw no point in unnecessary labour, but tried to arrange matters so that the citizens are left with plenty of time in which they may develop the full liberty of the mind and the furnishing of the same. For herein they suppose the felicity of life to consist.'[5]

Some three centuries after Sir Thomas More met his untimely end at the hands of King Henry VIII, John Stuart Mill pointed out the benefits that he considered likely to accrue from the emergence of a stationary state of economic development. Such benefits included:

'a much larger body of persons than at present, not only exempt from the

Unwin, 1985, p. 505.

5  T. More, *Utopia: Or, the Happy Republic*, Joseph Rickerby, 1838, p. 96.

coarser toils but with sufficient leisure to cultivate the graces of life.'[6]

Almost a century later, the English philosopher Bertrand Russell wrote an essay entitled *In Praise of Idleness* in the course of which he asserted that:

'a great deal of harm is being done in the modern world by the belief in the virtuousness of work [whereas] the road to happiness and prosperity lies in the organised diminution of work.'[7]

A generation later, in the high noon of the post–World War II full employment boom, J.K. Galbraith published *The Affluent Society*. Although more a criticism of the direction

6   J.S. Mill, *Principles of Political Economy*, University of Toronto Press, 1965, p. 755.
7   B. Russell, *In Praise of Idleness*, Unwin Paperbacks, 1984, p. 13.

economic growth was taking – private affluence amid public poverty – than of the idea of economic growth itself, the book included a chapter entitled 'Labour, Leisure and the New Class'. In the course of this chapter Galbraith argued that:

> 'over the span of man's history … ordinary people have never been quite persuaded that toil is as agreeable as its alternatives. Thus to take increased well-being partly in the form of more leisure is unquestionably rational.'[8]

---

8   Galbraith, op. cit., p. 256.

# CHAPTER 3

# TOWARDS
A LEISURE-
ORIENTED
SOCIETY

Fifteen years later, in a series of essays published under the title of *Toward a Steady-State Economy*, the idea of increased leisure as an alternative to the increased output of goods and services surfaced again. In his introduction to this collection of essays, the editor, H.E. Daly, while admitting that 'taking the benefits of technological progress mainly in the form of increased leisure was a reversal of ... historical practice',[9] goes on to quote Bertrand Russell's essay *In Praise of Idleness* with approval as representing a policy of 'leisure growth rather than commodity growth',[10] which will in turn provide opportunities for 'time intensive activities – friendship, care of the aged and children, meditation and reflection'.

Since the end of World War II, the 1973 publication of the series of essays grouped under the title of *Toward a Steady-State Economy*[11] was the only significant attempt made to present a coherent alternative to our present growth-oriented culture.

---

9   H. Daly, *Toward a Steady-State Economy*, H. Daly (ed.), W.H. Freeman & Co., 1973, p. 20.

10  Daly, op. cit., p. 21.

11  Daly, op. cit.

The concept of a steady-state economy reflected the current debate in astronomical circles about theories of the universe – big bang or steady state. The idea of a steady-state economy appealed to environmentalists, but once economists pointed out its implications – that it involved an end to further increases in goods and services available to the community – the concept disappeared into the warehouse of history. The concept of a steady-state economy can be presented in a more moderate form as a leisure-oriented economy. In such a situation the output of goods and services does not cease but leisure shares the position in the public agenda of working. Fortuitously 24 hours can be divided into 3 segments of 8 hours and 4 segments of 6 hours. The normal current practice is to work to the 8 hours standard and modify it by the use of casual labour to bring working times to 6 hours rather than 8. This in effect will allow for a four day working week.

For both sides of the labour market, the four day working week offers outstanding benefits. For the buyers of labour – aka employers – it offers the opportunity of levelling out the peaks and troughs in the supply and demand for labour which bedevil a modern complex economy. For the sellers of labour – aka workers or employees – it reduces their required working time.

They could either offer their services on a full-time or part-time basis to their existing or other employers, or they could accept the going rate of pay and concentrate on reducing their cost of living by exploiting the almost limitless rebates and discounts on every good and service available in the marketplace. It would give employees a freedom of choice and such freedom would represent a major advance in human welfare.

The idea of 'leisure only growth' is, of course, a somewhat extremist one. It can, however, be readily modified into the less absolute form of a 'leisure-oriented society'. In such a society, the idea of continuing economic growth need not be abandoned; the emphasis simply changes, from producing more to working less: from continually expanding the output of goods and services available for consumption to increasing the leisure time available to individuals for personal development.

By way of endorsement, the concept of a leisure-oriented society is compatible with the ideas of ten out of the eleven writers in *Toward a Steady-State Economy*.

To become a practical reality, however, a leisure-oriented society must first satisfy two prerequisites:

i.    i. It must be compatible with the perceived self-interest of the individual citizen.

ii.   ii. It must ensure that employment opportunities are comparable to those usually available in prosperous democratic economies.

A country boyhood instilled in the author an ongoing affinity for the environment. A teenage decision led to a working life involved directly or indirectly with economic affairs.

He has, however, never been able to share in the importance mainstream economists attach to economic growth.

There is an alternative: a leisure-oriented culture.

Vernon Routley